Be a City Nature Detective

Solving the Mysteries of How Plants and Animals Survive in the Urban Jungle

Text and Artwork by

Peggy Kochanoff

D1736822

NIMBUS
PUBLISHING
NIMBUS.CA

Nimbus Publishing Limited
3660 Strawberry Hill St., Halifax, NS, B3K 5A9
(902) 455-4286 nimbus.ca

Printed and bound in Canada

NB1336

Design: Jenn Embree

Library and Archives Canada Cataloguing in Publication

    Kochanoff, Peggy, 1943-, author, illustrator
    Be a city nature detective : solving the mysteries of how plants and animals survive in the urban jungle / Peggy Kochanoff.
    Issued in print and electronic formats.
    ISBN 978-1-77108-572-4 (softcover).—ISBN 978-1-77108-573-1 (HTML)
    1. Urban animals—Juvenile literature. 2. Urban plants—Juvenile literature. 3. Urban ecology (Biology)—Juvenile literature. I. Title.

QH541.5.C6K63 2018   j577.5'6   C2017-907977-8
                                             C2017-907978-

Nimbus Publishing acknowledges the financial support for its publishing activities from the Government of Canada through the Canada Book Fund (CBF) and the Canada Council for the Arts, and from the Province of Nova Scotia. We are pleased to work in partnership with the Province of Nova Scotia to develop and promote our creative industries for the benefit of all Nova Scotians.

Thanks to my wonderful family (Stan, Tom, Jim, Avai, and Jaya)
for all their support.

Thanks to Jim Wolford (retired biology teacher at Acadia
University) for checking my nature facts and wording.

Also, thanks to Nimbus Publishing for all their help and
encouragement and for making the process fun.

Introduction

City dwellers may not realize the number of plants and animals with which they coexist. Organisms have to be extremely tough to live in an environment with cars, people, pollution, noise, lights, concrete, dirt, and garbage surrounding them. The plants and animals that live in the city are truly remarkable, having adapted to these surroundings.

Most of the insects and animals discussed in this book are nocturnal, meaning they're active at night and not often seen in the daytime. Because they are **omnivorous**, they can eat just about anything and live just about anywhere. Many, like the red fox, have eyes that adapt to nighttime.

Several plants mentioned are **biennials**. A biennial's life cycle takes two years from seed to death, giving it a long time to establish. It has a deep **taproot** that stabilizes it and finds water when needed. Every biennial has a large number of seeds that spread long distances. Other plants, like dandelions, are **perennials**; these plants grow back year after year.

Luckily, many cities have public parks and green spaces and some city dwellers have gardens, making it easier to get closer to nature. Look around the city and you will be surprised by what nature you will find.

fox eyes, daytime

fox eyes, nighttime

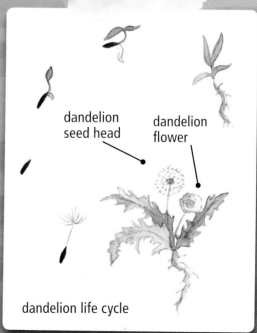

dandelion seed head

dandelion flower

dandelion life cycle

Look up definitions to words in **bold** in the glossary at the back of the book (starting on page 54).

Bedbugs

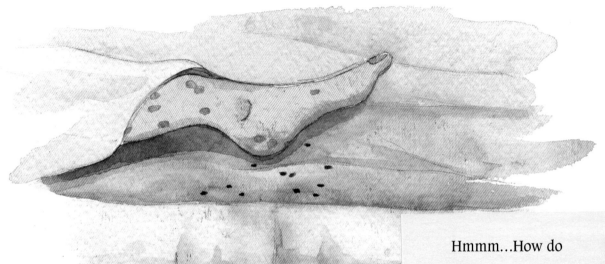

Hmmm...How do bedbugs get into your home?

Let's look closely and find out.

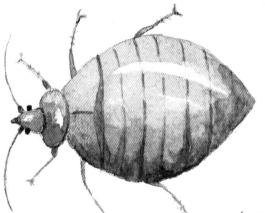

enlarged bedbugs
(actual size, 4.5 mm, or 1/5 inch)

Bedbugs enter homes in mattresses, bed frames, box springs, headboards, bedding, and luggage, and will lay hundreds of eggs. They are found in both clean and dirty rooms. Being flat and the size of apple seeds, they can creep into small and thin spaces easily. Immature, or **nymph**, bedbugs shed their skin five times before becoming adults and require a meal of blood before each shedding.

Bedbugs are parasitic, meaning they live off other organisms. They feed only on animal blood, but human blood is their favourite. While a person sleeps, the insect pierces the skin and sucks blood through an elongated beak for three to ten minutes. Once filled up, they scurry away unnoticed. Their bite is painless, but later, itchy welts form and turn red. Luckily, bedbugs don't spread diseases.

If you spot a bedbug, let your parents know right away! They are very difficult to get rid of.

Mystery solved!

Cockroaches

Hmmm…Do cockroaches
spread diseases?

Let's look closely
and find out.

From contaminated food, cockroaches spread bacteria and viruses that cause several sicknesses including salmonella (symptoms similar to food poisoning). Salmonella can remain in a cockroach's digestive system for up to a month and then be deposited in its droppings, urine, and vomit which can then pollute our food and water. Proteins in droppings, urine, saliva, vomit, eggs, and shed cuticles (the hard outer layer or shell) can cause allergic reactions in humans. They also give off a smelly secretion. Their varied diet includes baked goods, cheese, starch, glue, grease, wallpaper, soap, leather, hair, plants, paper, dirty clothes, tea, dead animals, sewage, and even other cockroaches. Yuck!

Unfortunately, cockroaches are hard to eliminate. The species is over 300 million years old, and when dinosaurs were wiped out, cockroaches survived. If there was a nuclear war, scientists think cockroaches would survive better than humans because they tolerate higher levels of **radiation**.

You are not likely to come across a cockroach because they are only active at night and avoid light. Being thin and flexible, they fit through tiny cracks and under doors, and with sticky feet they walk up walls and cupboards. Although they are icky, they are tough and fascinating.

Mystery solved!

Rats

Hmmm...Are rats in the city dangerous?

Let's look closely and find out.

Yes, there are many ways rats spread diseases. Their urine, droppings, and saliva can carry viral and **bacterial diseases**. Because rat-bite fever is caused by a bacteria in the mouth, nose, and respiratory tract, you could catch it from touching live or dead rats, but especially if you are bitten or scratched. Allergic reactions and asthma flare-ups can be caused by rat droppings, hair, and **dander**, which can also contaminate food and water. Fleas, lice, and mites living on rats also carry diseases. The most famous example is **bubonic plague**, a terrible outbreak carried by rat fleas that occurred in the fourteenth century in Europe, Africa, and Asia, killing 50 million people.

Like other rodents, a rat's incisors (sharp, cutting teeth at the front of the mouth) grow throughout its whole life, meaning it has to chew constantly to wear them down. Because rats gnaw through wire, wood, and plastics, they can cause structural damage to buildings. A hole the size of a quarter is big enough for some rats to squeeze through because parts of the skull are not fused together and can change shape.

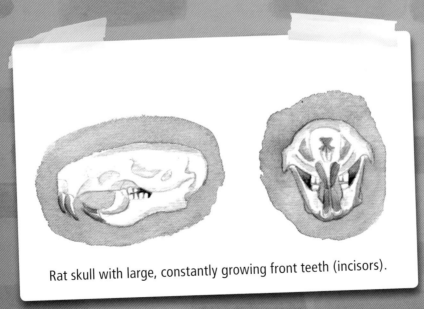

Rat skull with large, constantly growing front teeth (incisors).

Rats live in large groups, eating huge quantities of food and contaminating what is left. They are mainly active at night, scavenging around garbage bins and composters. These groups live in sewers, burrows, and tunnels.

If overcome by drainage, a rat can tread water for three days. Even though they only live an average of one year, they start mating at two to three months. Scientists think rats originated in China then followed human migration routes. With litter sizes averaging between eight to ten babies and with females able to have up to five litters per year, numbers are able to explode from just two rats to fifteen thousand in a year!

Rats have now spread to every continent except Antarctica. After humans, rats are the most successful mammal on earth, surviving anywhere humans do and thriving in large numbers.

A rat litter.

Mystery solved!

Grey squirrels

Hmmm…Why are some grey squirrels black?

Let's look closely and find out.

Black squirrels are just a **mutation** of a **gene** in grey squirrels. Mutation means there is a change in the structure of a gene and, in this case, the gene that controls colour. When old-growth forests with thick foliage were common, there were more black squirrels. They hid in the shade more easily than light-coloured squirrels, meaning more of the darker squirrels survived. Today, they aren't as common. However, in northern climates, their black colour absorbs more sunlight and warmth.

Grey squirrels are common in the city and find a variety of food: acorns, seeds, berries, tree buds, bulbs, insects, fungi, frogs, bird eggs, and bird-feeder food. They often bury nuts in the fall and smell or remember where the majority are.

Squirrels don't seem to mind humans but can be destructive if they get into your attic, cellar, or garage. When they need to escape, they are very fast, moving effortlessly through the trees using branches as pathways. The huge fluffy tail is used for balance as well as warmth, shade, a parachute, and, occasionally, to distract an enemy.

Mystery solved!

Red fox

Hmmm...Why is the red fox considered "cat-like?"

Let's look closely and find out.

While it is a member of the dog family (Canidae), the red fox has many cat-like features. Its oval pupils become slit-like (like cats) during the day to protect its light-sensitive eyes, then open wider to let more light in at night. Its claws are **semi-retractable**, so during hunting when traction is needed, the claws are out. They retract inward when not needed, preventing wear and keeping them sharp. Other members of the dog family, known as canines, always have their claws out.

The red fox's long, sensitive whiskers feel for prey and its teeth are thin and very sharp. It kills with one piercing bite instead of biting and shaking. When silently stalking prey, it freezes and pounces just like a cat.

Red foxes weigh only 4.5–5.4 kilograms (10 to 12 pounds) but their beautiful bushy coats make them look much larger. Humans should avoid contact especially if a fox is acting strangely. They can carry **rabies**, **mange**, and **distemper**.

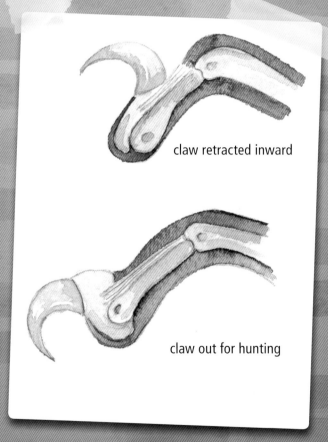

claw retracted inward

claw out for hunting

Red foxes survive quite well in the city and are heavier and healthier than rural foxes. Food is everywhere and they are omnivorous, meaning they eat almost anything: mice, voles, squirrels, birds, fruit, corn, amphibians, reptiles, insects, grubs, worms, **carrion**, and trash. Living closely with people doesn't seem to bother them.

Because red foxes prowl and hunt at night, they are rarely seen. Old buildings, alleys, culverts, golf courses, and green areas under power lines provide shelter and places to den. Besides getting hit by a car occasionally, their only city predator is the coyote.

Mystery solved!

Coyotes

Hmmm...Why don't people usually see coyotes in the city?

Let's look closely and find out.

Just because we don't often see coyotes in the city doesn't mean they're not there. Coyotes are extremely intelligent and wary of humans. They quietly prowl and hunt at night to avoid being seen. Although they have no predators, they are occasionally killed by cars.

Scientists have discovered city coyotes live longer than rural ones and in higher numbers. One big reason for their success is that they eat almost everything: rats, mice, rabbits, squirrels, birds, fruit, insects, garbage, and even pets and stray cats.

Coyotes will pounce, like foxes, especially when hunting small prey.

Eastern coyotes are larger than western coyotes, and DNA tests show they have wolf and dog genes in varying degrees. This happened in the past but there are no signs of it happening today. Coyotes, wolves, and dogs are similar enough to interbreed, but they would rather not and can more easily find their own type of mate.

Sometimes people try to eliminate coyotes by trapping, poisoning, or shooting them, but these animals are so cunning and adaptable that it doesn't work. When a coyote is removed from an area, a new one will move in. Females will also breed earlier and increase their litter size so numbers stay stable. They are the most widely distributed carnivore (meat-eater) in the **Western Hemisphere**.

western coyote

eastern coyote

Mystery solved!

Starlings

Hmmm...How do flocks of starlings fly and turn without bumping into each other?

Let's look closely and find out.

These shape-changing flocks are called **murmurations**. Hundreds, sometimes thousands, of birds move in one fluid motion. Scientists have determined that one bird's movement affects its seven closest neighbours, and that action spreads to each of those birds' seven nearest neighbours, and so on and so on. Watch for these beautiful moving shapes!

In fall, the starling's iridescent purple and green plumage becomes white-speckled like it has been snowed upon, and its yellow beak fades to grey. By February, many of the white-feather tips wear off and the bill becomes yellow again.

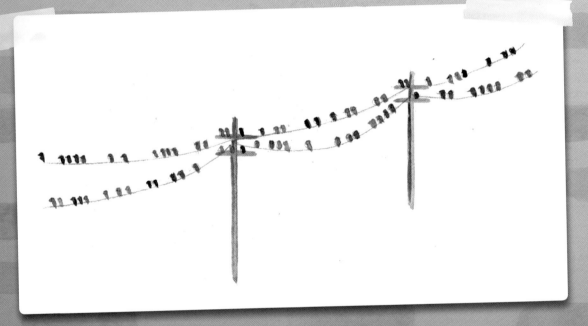

We've all seen starlings (and other birds) lined up on power lines. This is a wonderful way to look around for food sources and to see predators approaching. Have you wondered why they aren't electrocuted? Electricity occurs when electrons flow along the easiest path, in this case, the wire. Bird cells and tissues don't offer the electrons an easier route, so they continue along the wire and no shock occurs.

In 1890, sixty starlings imported from England were released in Central Park, New York City, by a man named Eugene Schieffelin. As a Shakespeare lover, Eugene wanted all the birds mentioned in the famous playwright's works to be introduced into his new country. (Starlings were mentioned in Shakespeare's play *Henry IV*.) Because starlings eat nearly everything (fruit, insects, worms, lizards, frogs, grain, and garbage), their numbers rapidly increased. Today there are over 200 million starlings from Alaska to Mexico, all from the original sixty!

Unfortunately, starlings have taken many nesting sites of North America's native birds, and sometimes even force birds out of their nests and eat their eggs and chicks.

Crops have been devastated by large flocks of starlings feasting on them, and starlings have even caused plane crashes. Where droppings collect, disease can spread, so beware. Luckily, starlings are easy to spot. If you have flocks roosting near your house, you will hear their loud, annoying squeaks, whistles, rattles, and even mimicry of the calls of other birds.

adult starling

Mystery solved!

Pigeons

Hmmm...Why are there so many pigeons in the city?

Let's look closely and find out.

Pigeons are also known as "rock doves" because they originally nested and roosted on rocky cliffs and ledges. Tall city buildings are perfect substitutes for nest sites. There is also a lot of food for pigeons in the city: seeds, insects, spiders, berries, scraps from people, plus people tolerate pigeons and love to watch and feed them, unlike they do other city animals such as rats and cockroaches.

There are three hundred varieties of pigeons and most are sooty grey. Light-coloured pigeons tend to be singled out by hawks and falcons (their main predators) because they are easier to spot. This is why there are fewer lighter ones compared to the darker greys.

While pigeons are not dangerous, their droppings are very acidic and will corrode brick, stones, and paint. Accumulations can irritate allergies and associated fungal spores can cause diseases. Fungal spores are microscopic particles that allow fungi to reproduce. Spores can cause a variety of diseases affecting your lungs, skin, intestines, and nervous system.

adult male pigeon with neck swelling

When attracting a mate, pigeons do a lot of bowing, scraping, cooing, and neck swelling.

A loose collection of twigs on a ledge serves as a nest for the couple.

When young hatch, both parents feed them with "pigeon milk." This milk is a thick, curd-like substance made in glands in the lining of the food storage chamber in their throat, known as a crop. It has a higher protein and fat content than human or cow milk. This is important, because milk higher in protein and fat helps increase a baby's growth rate and improves general health.

Mystery solved!

GULLS

Hmmm...Why aren't the gulls in the city out at sea?

Let's look closely and find out.

Usually the bird people call a "seagull" is the most common gull, the herring gull. It is pale grey on top of its back and white underneath and on the head, with pink legs and a yellow bill. **Juvenile** gulls take three or four years to achieve their adult colouration. Until then, they have messy looking darker brown and grey streaks. You might notice a red spot on the adult's yellow bill. When chicks peck at this spot, adults throw up partially digested food for babies to eat.

juvenile herring gull

Herring gulls do feed in open water and along the shoreline but are also found far inland near lakes, rivers, in plowed fields, mudflats, airports, parking lots, city rooftops, in garbage dumps, and looking for trash on the streets. Their diet is varied with fish, crabs, sea urchins, mussels, clams, snails, insects, worms, small mammals, eggs, trash, and carrion all working to fill their bellies.

Living in the city allows these birds to nest on the roofs of buildings. This way, they avoid a lot of predators and more young seagulls survive. The simple nest is a shallow depression lined with plants, feathers, or even plastic.

adult gull amongst the trash

Mystery solved!

Lichen

Hmmm…What are those strange splotches on buildings, trees, and stones?

Let's look closely and find out.

Each splotch is called lichen and is actually two organisms helping each other live, a phenomena called **symbiosis**. One is an alga, a simple green plant, making food by **photosynthesis**. The second is a fungus which provides a place to grow, collects water, minerals, wind-borne nutrients, and protects the alga from excess wind and sun.

Lichens are very important as pioneers in places where little life is growing. When they dry out, they shrink, pulling up the tiny bits of rock they live on. They also secrete acid that very slowly dissolves pieces of rock and forms hollows. However, they grow very slowly (1.3 cm or half an inch every year), so this process takes a very long time. Some lichens grow for four thousand years. Eventually, soil and air-borne seeds collect and higher plants begin to grow.

There are over fifteen thousand different kinds of lichens in many shapes, sizes, and colours.

British soldiers have hollow, erect stems with a red fruiting body on top that resembles a British soldier's hat.

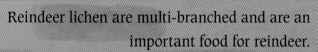

British soldiers

reindeer lichen

Reindeer lichen are multi-branched and are an important food for reindeer.

leafy lichens

Leafy lichens are crispy, brittle patches on rocks, trees, and the ground.

Lichens are exceptionally tough and grow from the Arctic to the Antarctic in conditions that are extremely hot to brutally cold (49°C to -18°C / 120°F to -4°F), under snow, in deserts, on rocks, and on trees. The only place you won't see lichens is where there is **air pollution** or **acid rain**. Lichens are very sensitive to toxins in the air, especially sulphur dioxide. Pollutants such as this destroy chlorophyll (the green pigment in plants responsible for absorbing the sun's light) so that photosynthesis can't occur.

Mystery solved!

ost people blame goldenrod for their hay fever, an inflammation in the nose caused by plant pollen, but ragweed is actually the culprit. Both plants bloom at the same time, late summer. But they are quite different.

Ragweed pollen is dry and dust-like and is blown in clouds by the wind. It has a rough outer shell that is very irritating to human membranes and can cause sneezing, a runny or swollen nose, and watery or swollen eyes.

Goldenrod pollen is sticky and heavy and isn't blown very far from the plant.

ragweed plant in flower

close-up of ragweed flowers

goldenrod plant in flower

close-up of a goldenrod flower

Several kinds of goldenrod are common in cities, growing in soil that is waterlogged or dry and usually in the sun rather than shade. After soil is disturbed, goldenrod is one of the first plants to grow. When it becomes widespread, other plants are kept out. There are over one hundred types of goldenrod and they are considered weeds all over North America; however, in Europe, people prize having them in their gardens. Enzymes in goldenrod will break down toxins in the soil, making it easier for plants to grow. Bees, wasps, butterflies, and flies are attracted to goldenrod's large quantities of nectar and pollen.

insects on goldenrod flower

A warm, moist cloth (poultice) with herbs, around a leg.

For many years, Indigenous people have used goldenrod to heal wounds. A tea has been used for ulcers, fever, kidney problems, and chest pains, and a **poultice** from boiled roots is helpful on burns and sprains.

Mystery solved!

Burdock seeds

Hmmm…How do burdock seed heads stick to us so tightly?

Let's look closely and find out.

Look closely at the seed head and you will see tiny hooks that catch in the loops in fabric. This is how the prickly seed heads attach to clothing and animal fur and are carried great distances. After seeing these tiny hooks, a Swiss engineer named George de Mestral invented Velcro. The word "Velcro" comes from the French *velour* (velvet) and *crochet* (hooks), thus, hooked velvet.

Burdock is a biennial. Over its two-year lifespan, one plant will release thousands of seeds which spread quickly into waste areas, old fields, sidewalk cracks, and river banks. These can grow to 1.5 metres (5 feet) with pink-lavender flowers blooming from July to October. Their nectar and pollen are very important to honeybees because clover flowers die off in August while burdock is still blooming.

Settlers brought burdock to North America for food and medicine, and now it is a widespread weed. The deep taproot (which may grow up to sixty-one centimetres or twenty-four inches) can be eaten like a root vegetable and tastes like parsnip. Burdock seeds, roots, and stalks have antioxidants, vitamins, and minerals to promote health.

seed head

hooks

flower head

Mystery solved!

Queen Anne's lace

Hmmm...What is the red spot in Queen Anne's lace?

Let's look closely and find out.

ach main bloom is formed from many individual, tiny florets. In the centre is usually one red-purple floret. Take a look! Scientists think it resembles an insect, which would attract other insects, which would then pollinate the flower. White flowers are **fertile**, meaning they will form seeds, but red ones aren't.

The intricate flower heads look very lacy, so the plant was named for the elaborate lace worn by royalty in the 1600s. According to "old wives' tales," Queen Anne pricked herself while making lace and a drop of blood formed this coloured flower, but this is just a fun story to tell!

red-purple floret

white florets

close-up of a spiny seed

Queen Anne's lace flower

dried flower head

Queen Anne's lace (also known as wild carrot) is a biennial and produces a **rosette** of leaves and an underground taproot during the first year. In the second year, a stalk grows with flowers. When the flower heads dry up, they look like little bird nests. Tiny bristly seeds with four rows of spines form. They easily catch on fur or clothing and blow long distances in the wind. One plant can produce forty thousand seeds which will live up to five years.

The plant is common in cities. Although preferring full sun, they are also found in partial sun. They grow in a variety of environments: clay, rocky, sandy, empty lots, and parks. The deep taproot anchors it securely and finds water in dry times.

Early settlers brought the plant to North America to use as a garden vegetable and for medicine. Seeds are good for flavouring soups and stews and are thought to relieve gas and **colic**. A tea made from the roots was traditionally used to settle digestive disorders and help with kidney and bladder diseases while strong boiled concentrations of roots and seeds could be used as an insecticide. Grated root was used to heal exterior wounds and internal ulcers.

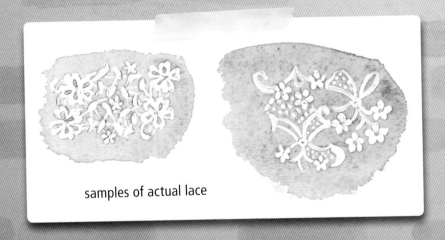

samples of actual lace

Mystery solved!

Dandelions

Hmmm...Why are dandelions so hard to eliminate?

Let's look closely and find out.

There are many reasons dandelions are so tough. Being perennials, they die back in fall but are alive underground over the winter. In spring, the plants start growing again and seem to pop up everywhere. Dandelions grow equally well in sun or shade. The deep taproot is hard to pull up and finds water when it's dry. The leaves grow in circular rosettes, keeping other plants from growing too close. Huge numbers of seeds are produced, and wind easily blows the little white parachutes far and wide. Whether you live in the country or city, you've had dandelions and you know how hard it is to get rid of them.

When brought to North America by homesick settlers, there were no diseases to keep dandelions in check, so their populations exploded. Luckily, they have some benefits. Young leaves gathered before flowers bloom can be eaten as salad greens and are full of vitamins. The taproot can be cooked and eaten as a vegetable or roasted and ground as a coffee substitute. Wine is made from flower heads, and green and yellow dye can be made from the flowers and leaves. Juice from the roots saved many lives from scurvy in years past.

Its name comes from the French "dent de lion" (lion's tooth) because of ragged edges on the leaves.

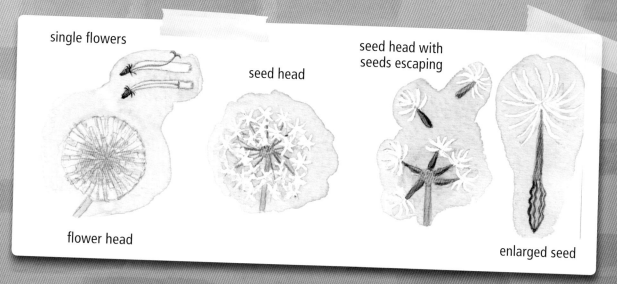

single flowers

seed head

seed head with seeds escaping

flower head

enlarged seed

Mystery solved!

Ginkgo tree

Hmmm...Why is the ginkgo tree called a "living fossil?"

Let's look closely and find out.

Fossils show that ginkgo trees were alive 270 million years ago in the era of dinosaurs. About 7 million years ago, they disappeared from fossil records in North America and 2.5 million years ago from fossils in Europe and were thought to be extinct; however, they actually survived in Chinese monasteries, temple gardens, and mountains. Buddhist monks cultivated them around 1100 AD, and seeds were transported to Japan and Korea. In 1691, Engelbert Kaempfer, a German physicist and botanist, discovered ginkgos in Japan and eventually they spread to Europe and North America.

Ginkgos adapt well to growing in the city because few insects attack them and they don't get many diseases. They are also resistant to wind and snow problems and tolerate pollution and small spaces. Ginkgos live very long and some are claimed to be 2,500 years old.

In the spring, the male and female buds look different from each other. The male buds look like tiny cones, while the female sends up slender green shoots with the leaves. Female buds eventually produce rounded pods filled with seeds.

female buds   male buds

Female trees drop fruit and are messy. When the fruit rots, some people say it smells like vomit or feces. Therefore, tidier male trees are planted along streets. The fruit of the ginkgo is edible, but the pulp has chemicals similar to poison ivy, making it very unpleasant to handle! You have to pull out the nut buried deep inside, dry, and roast it before it's edible. An extract from the leaves, called Ginkgo biloba, is sold as a dietary supplement to help brain function, memory, and blood pressure. However, scientists have not proven that it works.

female buds bearing fruit

Mystery solved!

Ailanthus

Hmmm...Why is Ailanthus called the "tree of heaven"?

Let's look closely and find out.

The name comes from the Alianthus's phenomenal ability to grow so quickly toward the sky. (During its first four years, this tree will grow an amazing 1–2 metres!) It is the fastest-growing tree or shrub in North America and was brought here from China. It will grow in pavement cracks, rubble, between bricks, train embankments, and vacant lots. Few insects or diseases attack it and it is one of the most pollutant-tolerant trees. To inhibit growth of competing nearby plants, a toxic chemical is given off by its roots, fallen leaves, and seeds into the soil.

In spite of these good points, many cities consider it very invasive, meaning it takes over its environment and negatively affects other vegetation. For this reason, it is not often planted anymore. **Suckers** sprout up from the roots, making it hard to ever get rid of them. The tree's strong roots can damage sewers, sidewalks, and building foundations. During storms, brittle stems may break off and litter streets. The tree also has an odd, stinky odour and has been called "stink tree."

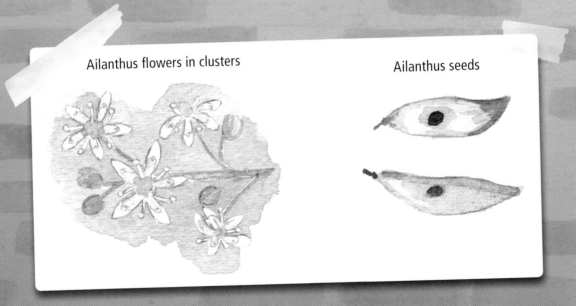

Ailanthus flowers in clusters

Ailanthus seeds

Mystery solved!

Night sky

country night sky

city night sky

Hmmm...Why is it so hard to see stars in the city?

Let's look closely and find out.

We need light to see, but in cities excess light creates light pollution. In rural areas, you should be able to see about 2,500 stars. In suburbs it is down to 200 or 300. Unfortunately, in the city you might only see a dozen or so stars.

City lights hit molecules in the air and are reflected back to your eyes. This is called "skyglow" and will drown out the light of stars. Your pupils need to be wide open at night to see stars, but all the city lights cause pupils to close, making it much harder to see them.

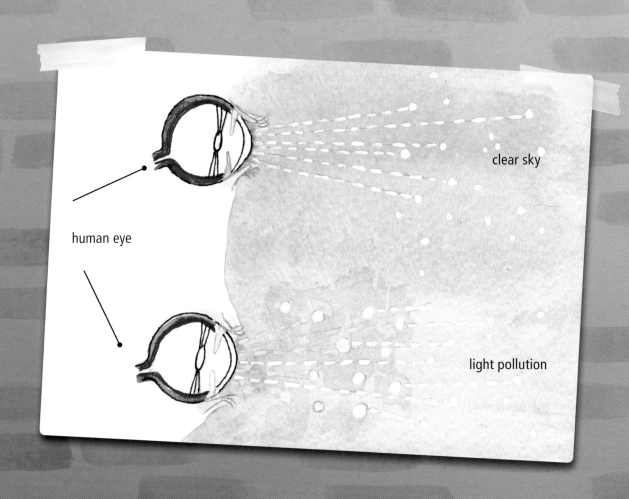

clear sky

human eye

light pollution

As you look around the city, you are probably surrounded by high buildings. This narrows the scope of sky and stars you see. In the country, unless surrounded by trees, you should see a wide horizon and many more stars.

Enjoy watching wherever you are, and also look for planets. Stars are far from Earth and their light is bounced around as it goes through our atmosphere, giving it a "twinkle" look. Planets are smaller and closer to Earth, so less light bounces and they don't appear to twinkle.

Mystery solved!

What can you identify?

murmuration

herring gulls

starlings-on-a-wire

grey squirrel

Queen Anne's lace

lichens

pigeons

dandelion plant and seeds

red fox

rat

Glossary

Air Pollution: Toxic compounds in the air that can be a health risk.

Acid Rain: When waste gases such as nitrogen oxide and sulfur are released when burning coal and fossil fuels and combine with water in the atmosphere, they increase the acidity of rain.

Bacterial Diseases: Infections caused by microscopic organisms.

Biennial: A plant taking two years to grow from seed to death.

Bubonic Plague: A contagious, often fatal, bacterial disease causing fever, chills, vomiting, and diarrhea. It is spread by flea bites (especially rat fleas) and by person-to-person contact.

Carrion: Decaying flesh of a dead animal.

Colic: Strong pain and discomfort in the stomach caused by intestinal gas, often found in young babies.

Dander: Loose cells and feather pieces shed from an animal that may cause an allergic reaction.

Distemper: A viral disease in some animals (especially dogs) causing fever, coughing, mucus discharge, and a lack of energy.

Fertile: Capable of producing offspring.

Gene: A complex unit passed on by a parent that determines characteristics in an offspring.

Juvenile: Young, immature.